PEACE POM

Ronan Makes a Difference

Written by **Mark Gruber-Lebowitz**

Illustrated by Sheldon Gruber-Lebowitz

For the dedicated peacemakers whose tireless efforts continue to inspire and motivate us toward working for peace and justice.

And for Norma, who never got a book.

To Susan
+
Larry~
Wage Peace!
Mark G L

Susan Amber Lebioda

AuthorHouse™
1663 Liberty Drive
Bloomington, IN 47403
www.authorhouse.com
Phone: 1 (800) 839-8640

Published by AuthorHouse 09/06/2018

ISBN: 978-1-5462-5855-1 (sc)
978-1-5462-5856-8 (e)

Library of Congress Control Number: 2018910396

Print information available on the last page.

Any people depicted in stock imagery provided by Getty Images are models,
and such images are being used for illustrative purposes only.
Certain stock imagery © Getty Images.

This book is printed on acid-free paper.

authorHOUSE®

Last year at this time, we began the process of creating a book about our wonderful dog, Ronan. We began that work blindly, not sure for quite a while whether we would see that project through to its completion. With the encouragement and support of many friends, One Lucky Pom: The Adventures of Ronan and His Dads did indeed find its way to publication. The positive response that first book received fueled our commitment to move forward with this second Ronan book.

Many thanks to all those who purchased and promoted our first book, via word of mouth and gift-giving.

Thanks as well to those who came out and attended our book signing events, adding to the festive joy of seeing this dream of publication come true.

Hello there, I'm Ronan, a wee Pom am I!
I'm a young Pomeranian pup, and I'll try
To explain why it matters each day without cease
That we all work together to make and keep PEACE.

There are all kinds of peace, and each one is the way
That we should be living our lives day by day.
We can all make a difference for good, yes it's true,
Making peace through the things that we say and
we do!

I will tell about peace that we carry inside,
Then I'll move on to kinds we can share far and wide.
So let me get started to tell what peace is,
And how to dive into the peacemaking biz!

Before spreading peace all around can begin
We must first find our own peace that lives deep
within.
If you're lucky, you know what brings peace to
your soul . . .
I mean peace like a river that makes you feel whole.

For me, I find peace when I run and I play,
Comfy grass 'neath my paws on a breezy fall day.
And sitting curled up on a warm, special lap
Also makes me a brimming-with-peace kind of chap.

Just to think of my friends brings me peace through
and through
As I picture the always-fun things that we do.
One more favorite thing that's within my mind's reach
Is watching the waves on my favorite beach!

Some peacemaking might seem incredibly small,
As if what you do makes no difference at all --
Like sharing the toy that's the one you love best,
Though you'd much rather keep it held tight to your chest.

And when a friend's hurting and you lend a hand
You're making a difference you can't understand.
In these gestures of kindness, you're waging real peace
That can make others' happiest feelings increase!

Feel the sadness in others and change it to joy,
Turning frowns upside down with each trick you employ . . .
Find a place of dark sadness, plant light in its place
Waging peace that this world can't destroy or erase!

Every once in a while a bully shows up
To make fun of or threaten an innocent pup.
This could happen to anyone, any old day,
At home or outside as you walk, work, or play.

If you see a bully who's not being nice,
Ask yourself right away without thinking twice
"Just what can I do to help bring to an end
The behavior that's hurting or scaring my friend?"

If it's safe to speak out and to get in-between,
Stand up for a friend and at once intervene.
Otherwise, find a grown-up to show and to say
That bullying's never - NOT EVER - okay!

Just like other animals -- yep, people, too,
Each dog is its own shape, its own size and hue.
Some are furry, some hairless, and some
in-between
While some aren't the cutest that you've ever seen.

And colors? Oh gosh, there's too many to name
Which I love 'cause it's boring to all be the same.
Poms are little so I live quite close to the ground,
But plenty of big dogs can also be found.

My friends are all different, which really is cool . . .
Hey, I heart diversity, I am no fool!
We all play together, we all get along,
It's our differences that make our friendships
so strong!

Peace comes when we open our hearts, paws, and hands
To pups and to people from all the world's lands.
No matter the reason they come here to live,
A genuine WELCOME's the best gift to give!

No pup is illegal, no way and that's it . . .
There's plenty of room - hey, we're ALL gonna fit!

So let's greet each poodle, each crested as well,
Each Chihuahua with Mexican stories to tell.

God made us and loves us, wherever we're from,
And God thinks judging others is all kinds of dumb.
So make peace and make friends when new neighbors appear,
Building bridges, not walls, shouting "I'm glad you're here!!!"

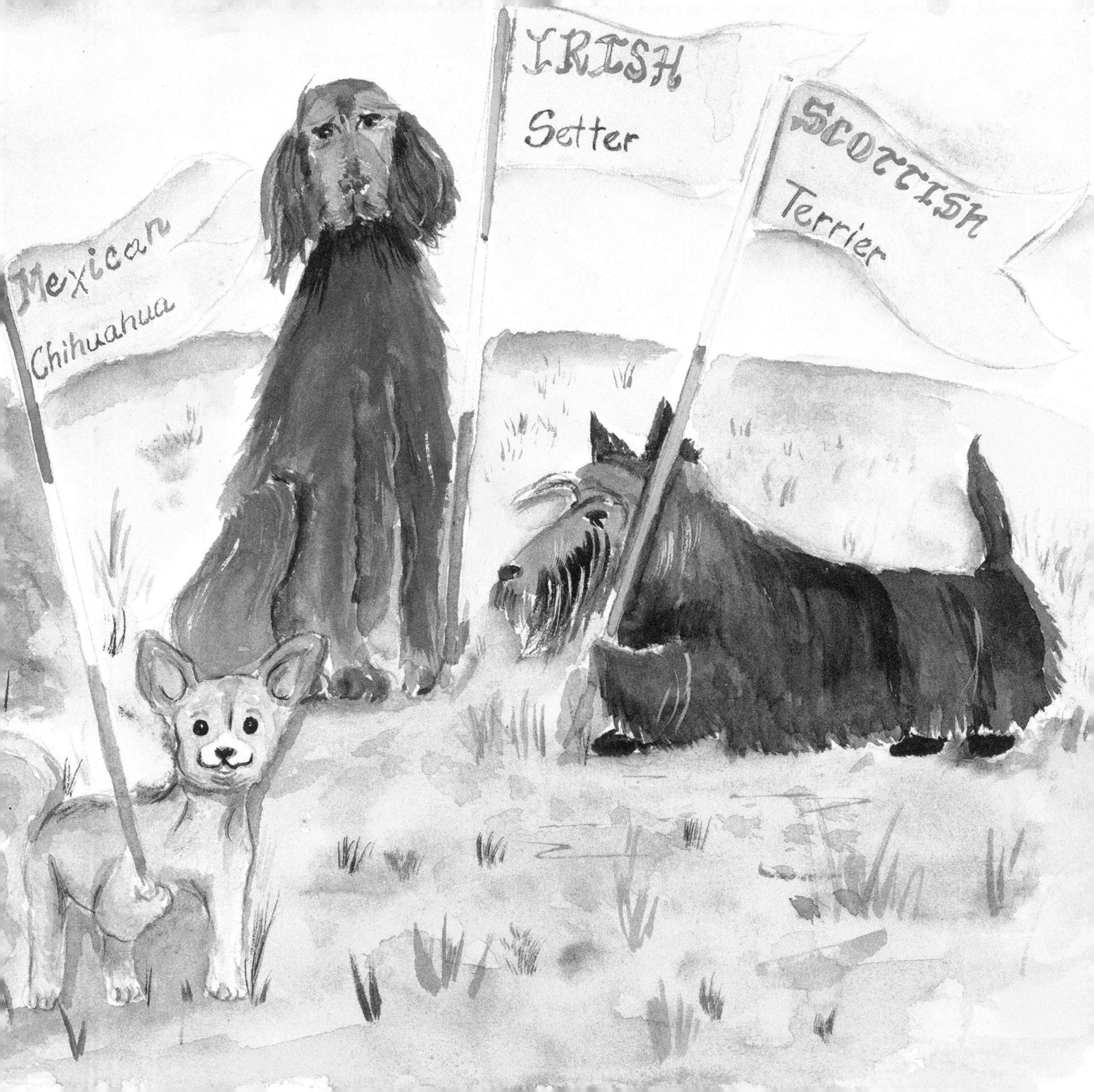
Mexican
Chihuahua
IRISH
Setter
Scottish
Terrier

Planet Earth is our home, it's where we all reside,
So peace comes with each bit of help we provide
To keep the Earth healthy and strong and like new . . .
That's one more type of peacemaking we can all do!

We can start just by picking up trash we may find
That's been tossed to the ground and then left behind.
Then we might clean the water for fish in the bay
Or use less electrical power each day.

Recycling, reusing, whatever we try
Will make this a healthier world by and by.
Give this wonderful planet your love and your care
As you tend to the land and the water and air!

There's one kind of peace that we all should strive for -
That's the peace that's the absence of violence and war . . .
Without any hitting or hurting we'd see
The way that our world was created to be.

Sometimes we get angry, that's normal to do,
But the trick is to know how to work anger through
Using words, not a fist or a paw or a gun
To get us right back to forgiveness and fun!

We're all children of God and that means, you see,
We're all of us part of the same family.
So as brothers and sisters, let's work night and day
To show that nonviolence is truly the way!!!

Sometimes a march is a good way to show
That justice and peace are the right way to go.
It's fun to go marching as part of a crowd . . .
Speaking up for what's right makes a peace pup
feel proud!

While marching for peace, you might walk
arm-in-arm
As you speak out against things that do the world
harm.
You might carry a sign with the message you bring
Or use words of a song, lifting voices to sing.

Whatever you do, march the peaceable way
So that others may see you and maybe they'll say,
"I agree with your sign and the words of your song,
And if there is room, I just might march along!"

So . . .

May the good that we do in this world never end
As we march and we sing and turn stranger
to friend.
And here's what we'll do, hand-in-hand, you and me:
work for justice,
be kind,
make

Dear Reader,

On these pages, it's dogs that have modeled the way
To make peace, and to spread it around every day.
But guess what: people too, whether little or tall,
Can be makers of peace in ways both big and small.

Yes you, whether you're still a child or all grown,
Can make peace in cool ways you have found on
your own.
If you do, spread the word so that others can find
New ways to live lives that are peaceful and kind.

Well, so long, now I'm off to find new things to do
That can help this old world that we're all passing
through;
We can do it together, have faith and be calm.
Love from Ronan, your buddy, the little peace Pom!

CPSIA information can be obtained
at www.ICGtesting.com
Printed in the USA
BVHW02s0355200918
527492BV00035B/97/P

9 781546 258551